Freedom Fighters

Withdrawn

Malcolm X

Mark Falstein

Globe Fearon Educational Publisher
Paramus, New Jersey

Paramount Publishing

Freedom Fighters

Cesar Chavez
Fannie Lou Hamer
Martin Luther King, Jr.
Malcolm X
Nelson Mandela

Editor: Tony Napoli
Production editor: Joe C. Shines
Cover and text design: London Road Design
Production: ExecuStaff

Photographs: Cover, pp. 14, 30, 45, 59, 66—UPI/Bettmann Newsphotos;
pg. 43—AP/Wide World Photos

ISBN 0-8224-3224-2

Printed in the United States of America

4. 10 9 8 7 6 5 4 3 2
MA

Contents

CHAPTER 1
Caged

He was handcuffed. And, as he was led toward the steel door, the rage and terror rose within him. How had it come to this? he wondered. Most criminals know that sooner or later they'll get caught. But he never really thought it could happen to him. He was too sharp. He could talk his way out of anything. That was how he had stayed alive on the streets of Harlem. He'd lived by his wits and his guts, gambling, stealing, selling drugs. He was "Detroit Red," a prince among hustlers.

All that was over now. The dope, the music, the women . . . the *life*. Here he wasn't "Detroit Red." Here he was only a number. When the cell door clanged shut behind him, Malcolm Little was just another prisoner.

Charlestown State Prison had been built in 1805. The cells had no running water. The toilet was a covered bucket. Lying on his cot, Malcolm could touch both walls. Ten years, he thought. *Ten years* in this . . . cage.

And for what? Usually, someone convicted of burglary as a first offense received a sentence of about two years. In his case, the rest of the sentence was for his real "crime": being with a white woman. His own lawyer had admitted as much. "You had no business with white girls!" the lawyer had said, his face red.

Malcolm did not take easily to prison. The sight of bars made him crazy. He threw things out of his cell and dropped his tray in the dining hall. He refused to answer when his number was called. He cursed the guards and other prisoners alike. Any talk about religion and the Bible brought on the loudest curses. The prisoners had their own name for him. They called him "Satan." Malcolm didn't care. He wanted nothing to do with anyone. He preferred the solitary confinement his behavior often earned him. In solitary, he would pace like a caged animal, bitter, as he thought about his life . . .

Malcolm Little's earliest clear memory was of fire and fear. He was a boy of four in East Lansing, Michigan. His father had shot at two white men who had set his house on fire. His mother, holding Malcolm's baby sister, just made it outside before the house fell in. Police and fire-men stood by, watching it burn.

It was not the first time white men had come after his father. Big Earl Little was a Baptist preacher. He was also an organizer for the Universal Negro Improvement Association. The UNIA's leader, Marcus Garvey, talked about building an independent black nation in Africa. He urged black people to stop trying to act like whites and to take pride in their own culture. Proud black men were scary to many whites. Earl Little had been run out of Omaha, Nebraska, for his UNIA work. Hooded riders of the Ku Klux Klan smashed the windows of his house while he was away. They warned his pregnant wife, Louise, that he had better leave town. The family left Omaha shortly after Malcolm was born, on May 19, 1925.

The Littles were a large family. Malcolm was the fourth of eight children. In Michigan, they had a small farm. They needed the vegetables and chickens they raised to add to Earl's income. Earl spent most of his time organizing meetings for the UNIA. Malcolm remembered going to those meetings. He remembered pictures of Garvey in a uniform and a song people would sing: "Up you mighty race, you can accomplish what you will."

One evening in 1931, Earl Little left the house after an argument with his wife. Hours later, he was found dead on the trolley tracks in town. His head had been beaten in, and a train had run over him. He had apparently been placed on the tracks after the beating and left to die.

The life insurance company didn't see it that way. It claimed Earl Little had committed suicide. The company refused to pay off on a policy Earl had taken out on himself. From then on, the Littles struggled. Malcolm's oldest brother, Wilfred, quit school to go to work. His oldest sister, Hilda, took care of the children while their mother looked for work. But Louise Little had never worked outside her home before. She couldn't find a steady job. Sometimes she found work cleaning houses or sewing clothes. Since she was light-skinned, people often thought she was white. When employers learned that she was black, she was usually fired. She became more and more depressed. Finally, she was forced to apply for welfare.

Poverty and welfare began to eat away at the family. Malcolm began hanging out with a crowd that made trouble and played pranks on local farmers. He soon began stealing as well. The welfare workers thought he was a bad influence on his brothers and sisters. They wanted him put in a foster home. Malcolm was already spending a lot of time at the home of a black family named Gohannas. They agreed to take him in.

Louise Little hated the welfare workers. As Malcolm would later write, they had no respect for her feelings. They invaded her privacy and set her children against one another. They called her "crazy" for refusing a butchered pig offered her by her neighbors. They didn't care that Mrs. Little had joined the Seventh-Day Adventists, a church whose members do not eat pork. In fact, Louise Little *was* losing her mind. Her despair was too much for her. She began talking to herself, and became almost unaware of her children. In 1937, she was put into a mental hospital. Her children were separated. Most of them were sent to foster homes.

Malcolm's anger and bitterness came out in school. Everyone could see how intelligent he was. But he was always "cutting up" in class and showed no respect for his teachers. The state decided to send him to reform school. First they sent him to a detention home located in the town of Mason, a few miles from Lansing. A white couple named Swerlin ran the home. They were "good people," Malcolm later said. They liked him. The Swerlins arranged it so that he didn't have to go to reform school. He stayed on at the detention home and went to Mason Junior High.

Malcolm was 13 that year. He looked older. He ranked third in his class and was popular among the other students. They asked him to join the debate club, the basketball team, and other activities. They elected him class vice-president. Malcolm felt that the reason he was popular was because he was the only black student in the class, something odd like a "pink poodle." It didn't bother him very much that some students and teachers called him "nigger." The Swerlins used the word too. They didn't mean any harm by it. Besides, Malcolm admitted, he was trying hard to be "white" in every way he could.

That all ended in the eighth grade. One day, a teacher asked Malcolm what he wanted to be when he grew up. Malcolm hadn't really thought about it much. "A lawyer," he finally answered. The teacher's reply shocked him. "That's no realistic goal for a nigger," he said kindly. He suggested Malcolm try a trade, such as carpentry.

From that day forward, Malcolm began to change. He knew the teacher had only been trying to help him. But he realized that white people would never accept him as an equal. He could be the best at everything, but he could get just so far in their world. He would always be "just another nigger."

He stopped caring about school. He drew away from the Swerlins and began to avoid white people. He had been working for a year washing dishes in a restaurant and had money to spend. He passed more and more of his time "hanging out" in Lansing's black district.

Malcolm had spent the previous summer in Boston, Massachusetts, visiting his half-sister, Ella Collins. She was Earl Little's daughter from an earlier marriage. Now Ella arranged to become his guardian. In 1940, soon after his 15th birthday, Malcolm took a bus to Boston.

He couldn't have been happier. He would later call Ella the first proud black woman he had ever known. She was a successful businesswoman. She owned a house on "the Hill." This was a wealthy section of Roxbury, the black district of Boston.

Ella urged Malcolm to explore the city. She thought he should get to know Boston before he took a job. He discovered historic Boston, where the American Revolution had begun. In a park was a marker honoring Crispus Attucks. Malcolm was surprised to learn that a black man had been the first to fall in the Boston Massacre. At school, black history had been one paragraph in a textbook. Malcolm was curious about everything. He explored the port area and the railroad stations. He took a subway one day and ended up at Harvard University.

What most fascinated him, however, was Boston's street life. He was drawn to the black slums with their bars and poolrooms. Here were young men who seemed to live without working. They dressed sharply, in zoot suits and flashy shoes. Their hair was shiny and straight like white peoples', a style Ella told him was called a "conk." They talked an exciting language Malcolm had never heard before. Men were "cats." Women were "chicks." A job was a "slave." Any way to make money without one was a "hustle."

Malcolm had already come to disrespect Ella's neighbors on the Hill. Most of them pretended to be more than they were. Someone who worked as a janitor in a bank might say he was "in banking." Malcolm found the street life far more appealing. He wanted to be a "hip cat," as the young men on the streets called each other.

In a pool hall, Malcolm met a hip cat called Shorty. He turned out to be from Lansing. Malcolm was soon spending his evenings with Shorty and his friends. They had no idea how young he was. Before his 16th birthday, he was well acquainted with liquor, drugs, and gambling.

Shorty was happy to help a "homeboy." He got Malcolm a "slave" shining shoes at Roseland, Boston's biggest dance hall. In the 1940s, jazz was king. Malcolm loved this music that his people had created. All the best bands played Roseland—Duke Ellington, Count Basie, Lionel Hampton. Malcolm bought a zoot suit. He conked his hair. It was a painful process that involved rubbing lye into his scalp. But now he belonged. He learned a lively style of shining shoes. He could make the rag pop like a firecracker. It earned him good tips from customers and musicians.

"Just remember, everything in this world is a hustle," one of his new friends told him. Malcolm learned this lesson well. Soon he was making extra money selling "reefer"—marijuana—and setting up white customers with black prostitutes.

Malcolm was surprised to see "mixed" couples walking together openly in Roxbury. He knew that male-female involvement across the "color line" was a forbidden, secret thing. Nothing made white men crazier than the thought of "their" women with black men.

Malcolm soon quit his job. He wanted to have his nights free to experience life. He wanted to dance at Roseland instead of shining shoes there. He got a job as a soda-fountain clerk at a drugstore in Ella's neighborhood. This pleased his sister, who was worried about the kind of people he was meeting.

At the drugstore, Malcolm met a young woman named Laura. She was a proper church-going girl. She came from a well-to-do African American family and planned to go to college. She loved to dance, and she was good at it. Malcolm took her to Roseland, but he never introduced her to his friends there. They would not understand each other, he decided.

They had not been dating very long when Malcolm met another woman at the dance hall. Sophia was cool, sophisticated, beautiful—and white. She was a status symbol for him. He began showing her off to his Roxbury friends. He stopped seeing Laura.

On December 7, 1941, Japanese planes bombed Pearl Harbor, Hawaii. The United States was plunged into World War II. Millions of young men joined the armed forces. Many jobs opened up. A friend of Ella's worked for a railroad. He told her he could get Malcolm a job if he could pass for 21. Malcolm was six feet, three inches tall. When he lied about his age, no one questioned him. Soon he was selling sandwiches on the Yankee Clipper, a train that ran daily between Boston and New York.

For some time now, Malcolm had wanted to get to New York City. He particularly wanted to visit Harlem. This huge section of the city was home to more black people than anyplace else in the country. He remembered his father showing him pictures of Marcus

Garvey's followers in Harlem marching in parades. Any time heavyweight boxing champion Joe Louis won a fight, the African American papers would carry pictures of cheering Harlem crowds.

On his first run to New York, Malcolm was taken to Harlem by other members of the train crew. Within minutes, Malcolm Little knew he'd found his home.

CHAPTER 2
"Detroit Red" in Harlem

One of the convicts in prison in Charlestown was a man called Bimbi. He and Malcolm worked together making license plates in the prison workshop. Bimbi was a thief. He had spent many years in prison. He'd used his time behind bars reading and studying. Malcolm had never met anyone who could command such respect with his words. When Bimbi talked, other prisoners listened. Even the guards paid attention.

One day, Malcolm heard Bimbi talking about religion. After that day, Malcolm stopped being "Satan." He still had no use for religion. But his curse-filled attacks ended. They sounded weak next to Bimbi's reasoned arguments. He sought Bimbi's friendship. "You've got some brains, if you'd use them," the older convict told him. There were correspondence courses available to prisoners. There was also the prison library. Bimbi urged Malcolm to take advantage of them.

Malcolm had little else to do with his time. He began to study. "The streets had erased everything I learned in school," he would later write. But he soon mastered English grammar and started to learn Latin. And he began to think about his life as a young black man in America. He was used to thinking of little but himself. But now he wondered about the social forces that had led him to wind up in prison. How had he chosen to follow the hustler's life? . . .

Soon after Malcolm began working for the railroad, he moved out of Ella's house. He rented a room in Harlem. The place hypnotized him. The nightlife was more exciting than he had imagined. He became a regular at the Savoy Ballroom. He went to shows at the Apollo Theater. He hung out at bars called Small's Paradise and the Braddock. He admired the hustlers who drank there. They were smooth. Before long, they knew who he was. They called him "Red" for his bright red conk. Because few of them had heard of Lansing, Michigan, Malcolm told people he came from Detroit. In time, he become known as "Detroit Red."

On the Yankee Clipper, he was called "Sandwich Red." He sold food as fast as the railroad could supply it. He discovered that if he put on a show for the white folks, he could sell them anything. Only years later did he realize he'd been acting like a clown. Often he was high on marijuana. The drug made him careless. After a while, his "show" crossed over into insult. Passengers complained about him. It wasn't long before he was fired.

Malcolm returned to Michigan to visit his brothers and sisters. In his zoot suit and conk, he seemed to them like a man from outer space. He stopped in to see his former foster family, the Swerlins. Mrs. Swerlin was so uncomfortable that Malcolm cut the visit short.

Back in Harlem, Malcolm needed a job. He was hired as a day waiter at Small's Paradise. Ed Small and his brother Charlie owned the bar. Ed told him the rules: no lateness, no laziness, no stealing. He knew Malcolm admired the hustlers he saw in his place. There was to be no hustling of the customers, he warned, especially not of servicemen.

For Malcolm, working at Small's was like being in school—a hustler's school. Every kind of hustler came to the bar. He learned everything he could about their hustles. There were gamblers, burglars, pickpockets, drug dealers, and stick-up men. Malcolm learned which hustlers were show-offs and which were truly dangerous. And he learned the most important rules of hustling: never trust anyone outside your own circle, and take time and care in choosing your circle.

He broke those rules only once. A black soldier came into Small's. He looked so lonely and so dumb sitting

Night life in Harlem during the 1940s—zoot suits, jitterbug dancing, and jazz—was more exciting than "Detroit Red" could have ever imagined.

there that Malcolm asked him if he wanted a woman. When the soldier said yes, Malcolm gave him the phone number of a prostitute. The soldier turned out to be a spy for the military police.

Malcolm was lucky that time. He had no police record. And he hadn't accepted money from the soldier. This suggested that he had only wanted to do the man a favor. The police turned him loose. But he was fired from his job at Small's. Worse, the Small brothers barred him from the club.

From then on, he decided, he would live only by hustling. There were eight million people in New York City. Malcolm figured that only half of them worked for a living. The other half lived by their wits. He would be one of those.

He started selling marijuana to musicians. About half the jazz musicians that came through Harlem used it. He knew so many of them that finding customers was easy. He would clear $50 or $60 a day—very good money in 1943. Before long, the police were after him. But he had ways to avoid getting caught. He moved from place to place, always staying one jump ahead of the law. He knew how to hide his "sticks" so that the police wouldn't find them if they searched him. He sold reefer in the poorest part of Harlem. His customers were people who stayed high much of the time to escape the misery of their lives.

About this time, Malcolm was called up before his draft board. Being drafted into the army was one of the three things he feared most, along with jail and having to find a job. He went to the army induction center in his wildest zoot suit. He was high. He talked a stream of loud and crazy slang. He told an army doctor that he hoped to organize black soldiers to rise up and kill whites. The doctor dropped his pencil. Malcolm Little was declared unfit for military service.

He was not fit for much of anything else by then, either. He tried to survive through small-time robbery. He had to be high to calm his fear. He began collecting bets for West Indian Archie, a numbers runner. "The numbers" was a lottery game played mostly by poor blacks. It was a chump's game. A winning number paid 600-to-1, but the real odds were 1,000-to-1. The only people who came out ahead were the hustlers who ran the game. Malcolm worked for West Indian Archie, but he also bet heavily on the numbers himself.

He was getting more and more out of control. He barely escaped with his life when one of his robberies was stopped by armed guards. Another time, he was "taken out" by white gangsters who thought he had robbed one of their dice games. Only the chance appearance of a police officer saved his life.

Finally, he even got into an argument with West Indian Archie, who accused him of cheating on a bet. Only $300 was involved, but neither man would back down. It was a matter of respect and reputation. Friends had to step in to prevent a shoot-out. Malcolm was now on the run from the police, from the mob, and from Archie. His friends warned him to leave town.

One day, a car drew up alongside him. "Hey, home-boy," someone called. Malcolm drew his gun. He almost shot the driver. It turned out to be Shorty, his friend from Boston. He had heard about Malcolm's troubles and had come to take him away from Harlem for a while.

Back in Roxbury, people were troubled by how he had changed. His talk now was all swearing or street slang. His sister Ella was bothered by how bad he had become. He disrespected women and sneered at religion.

Shorty had become a fine saxophone player. He played at small jazz clubs around Boston. Even he was disturbed by the changes in Malcolm. He seemed like an animal. Shorty had introduced him to reefer years ago. Now he was on drugs all the time—cocaine, benzedrine, opium.

Malcolm met Laura again. Sadly, this once proper, religious girl was now living more like Malcolm. She had dropped out of school. She spent her time taking drugs and partying. She and Malcolm got high together.

Sophia was around too. She and Malcolm had never really stopped seeing each other. She would come to New York on the train from time to time. Now she helped Malcolm cook up a new hustle. Shorty, Sophia's sister, and a man named Rudy were in on the plan. The two women went to homes in rich neighborhoods posing as saleswomen and survey takers. Once inside, they would get around the house as much as they could, spotting where valuables were kept. They'd draw a plan of the house. Then some evening, the men would burglarize the place.

At first, everything went smoothly. The gang pulled off one job after another. Then one day, Malcolm took a watch he had stolen to a jewelry store to be repaired. The watch had been reported to the police as stolen. Jewelers had been alerted.

Police detectives stepped out of the back of the store. Malcolm was arrested. Sophia and her sister were picked up that evening. Shorty was pulled out of the club where he was playing and taken to jail. Only Rudy was able to escape.

The two women were given light sentences. They were "nice white girls" from good families. Their worst crime was being involved with black men. Malcolm and Shorty each got ten years.

In February 1946, Malcolm Little began serving his sentence at Charlestown State Prison. He was not yet 21 years old.

CHAPTER 3
The Lost-Found Nation

Slowly, Malcolm adjusted to prison life. Using his mind helped tremendously. He also got some hustles going. He won cartons of cigarettes playing dominoes and sold them to the other prisoners. He booked bets on fights and baseball games.

In 1948, Malcolm was transferred to Concord State Prison. It was newer than Charlestown, and it had a better library. That same year, he received a letter from his brother Philbert in Detroit. Philbert wrote that he had discovered the "natural religion for the black man." He had joined "the Nation of Islam." He urged Malcolm to "pray to Allah for deliverance."

Malcolm was not moved. It seemed Philbert was always joining something. The year before it had been the Holiness Church. Malcolm still hated religion. He wrote back a nasty reply.

Then he got a letter from his brother Reginald. It was full of family news. But it also contained an odd statement. "Malcolm, don't eat any more pork and don't smoke any more cigarettes," Reginald wrote. "I'll show you how to get out of prison."

Malcolm did not connect the two letters. He had no idea what Reginald was getting at. *Get out of prison. . . .* It had to be some kind of hustle. If he quit eating pork and quit smoking, maybe he would be able to claim a health problem that would get him free.

Malcolm smoked four packs a day. But after he finished the pack he was working on, he never touched another cigarette. The next time pork was served in the dining hall, he refused it. Later, he would learn a saying: "If you take one step toward Allah, Allah will take two steps toward you."

The next word from Reginald came after Malcolm had been transferred again. Now he was at Norfolk Prison Colony. This facility was "heaven," as far as prisons went. It was located in the country. The prisoners lived in "houses" of 50 men each, and each man had his own room. There was a fine education program, with classes taught by university professors. A rich man had willed the prison his library, and it contained many books on history and religion. And visitors were allowed almost every day.

Reginald came from Detroit for a visit. It had been a long time since his "no pork or cigarettes" letter.

Malcolm was bursting with curiosity. But he let Reginald take his time. And what Reginald told him changed his life forever.

God's true name is Allah, Reginald said. At once Malcolm made the connection with Philbert's letter. Allah had come to America and made himself known to a man, "a black man like us." This man's name was Elijah Muhammad, and he lived in Chicago. Allah had told him that the devil's time on earth was up. The devil is a man, Reginald said. He is the white man. He is *all* white men. The white man *is* the devil.

At this point, we must interrupt Malcolm's story for some facts about "The Lost-Found Nation of Islam."

Islam is a worldwide religion. Its name is an Arabic word meaning "submission"—submission to the will of God. Its followers are called Muslims—"they who submit." The religion was preached by the prophet Muhammad during the seventh century in the country now called Saudi Arabia. Over the next few centuries, Muslims took over much of Asia, Africa, and southern Europe. Today, there are about 900 million Muslims. They are of all races, and they live in nearly every country on earth.

Islam teaches belief in one god. Muslims call him Allah, the Arabic word for "God." The religion teaches prayer, honesty, kindness, charity to the poor, and other practices common to many religions. Its teachings are written in a book called the Koran. Islam respects Jews and Christians for believing in one god and a holy book. It teaches that Jesus, Moses, and other figures of the Bible were prophets of Allah. Muslims are forbidden to eat pork, like Jews and some other religious groups. Muslims are also forbidden to drink alcohol and to gamble. They believe that people who properly submit to the will of Allah will be rewarded in heaven.

In 1930, a man named W. D. Fard, or Farrad, appeared in the black slums of Detroit. He was a silk salesman, possibly an Arab immigrant. He claimed to be from Mecca, Saudi Arabia, the holy city of Islam. He drew a group of followers who believed he was a wonder worker. Among the wonders he said he could work was to destroy white America.

One of Fard's ministers was an autoworker named Elijah Poole. Fard told Poole that he, Fard, was Allah come into the world. He said he had come to rescue the "lost-founds," as he called them—the black people in America. Fard taught Poole an odd mixture of traditional Islam and other ideas. Black people, he said, were the original humans. Black scientists built a mighty civilization. They created all the animals and raised mountains. They dug the moon out of the earth and communicated with people on Mars.

Then, Fard said, a scientist named Yacub created a devil race—the white man. They were a weak, mutant, bleached-out people. They lived in caves and went about on all fours, like dogs. But God had given these blue-eyed devils power over the world. They committed horrible crimes. The worst of these was the enslavement of black Africans—the tribe of Shabazz. This was the name of one of God's scientists. Shabazz had led the people into Africa 50,000 years ago to toughen them up for the devil's rule. The devil stole their language, culture, and religion. He corrupted them with his filthy ways and his "spook religion"—Christianity. There was no heaven or hell. The white man enjoyed heaven here on earth, and his heaven was the black man's hell. This hell had lasted 400 years, but now the devil's time was almost up.

Fard gave Poole a new name, Elijah Muhammad. He taught him that "Poole" was a slave name, the name of a devil who had owned his ancestors. In 1934, Fard mysteriously disappeared. Elijah Muhammad won a struggle with other ministers to become the leader of "The Lost-Found Nation of Islam in the Wilderness of North America." By 1949, it had a few hundred members, mostly in Detroit and Chicago. They turned their backs on white America and took pride in all that was black. They dressed neatly, worked hard, and formed a close community. They had their own schools and stores. They followed the teachings of Islam as interpreted by Mr. Muhammad. They were not supposed to smoke, drink, gamble, eat pork, or be unfaithful in marriage. These were the devil's ways.

Malcolm was confused by much of what Reginald said. But that one thought would not leave his head: *The white man is the devil.* Malcolm thought about the white people he had known. The men who had burned down his house. The men who had killed his father. The welfare workers who had called his mother "crazy" to her face. The judge who had broken up their family. The Swerlins. The teacher who had told him to forget about being a lawyer. The customers at Roseland. Sophia. The people he had worked for. The gangsters. The cops. His lawyer . . .

"You don't even know who you are," Reginald told him the next time he visited. "We're a race of kings. We invented civilization. The white devil has hidden our own history from us. We have been his victim ever since he murdered and raped and stole us from our own land."

Several of Malcolm's brothers and sisters had joined the Nation of Islam. Every day he received letters from them. They urged him to submit to Allah. They urged him to accept the teachings of the Honorable Elijah Muhammad. Sometimes the letters contained printed literature on these teachings. Black people in America, Muhammad taught, were the only race on earth that did not know their true identity. They didn't know their true family names. The "so-called Negro" was "a rape-mixed race." He had been told that Africa was a savage, backward place. He had been brainwashed into obeying, even worshipping, the white man. He had been taught to worship an alien god with the devil's white skin. He had been taught that everything black was a curse and everything white was to be admired. He had been taught to hate everything black, including himself. He had been taught to accept whatever the white man gave him. He had been taught to pray for heaven when he died, while the white devil had *his* heaven here on earth.

All this struck Malcolm like a blinding light.

He wrote to Elijah Muhammad in Chicago. It took him 25 tries to write a letter he wasn't ashamed to send. Allah's Messenger sent him a typed reply. He welcomed him to "true knowledge." He enclosed a five-dollar bill. He often sent money to black prisoners, as Malcolm would later learn. Muhammad wrote that the black prisoner was a symbol of the white man's crime. The devil kept blacks ignorant and poor. Unable to get decent jobs, they became criminals.

They became "Detroit Red."

Now Malcolm felt shame for the sinful life he had lived. But that shame prepared him to accept Mr. Muhammad's teachings.

He began to pray. He later described it as the hardest thing he had ever done. But in time, the worship of Allah became a joy to him. It lifted from his spirit the pain of remembering what he had been. He wrote to Mr. Muhammad every day. He received wonderful, inspiring letters in reply. He wrote to every hustler he had known, telling them about Mr. Muhammad's message. None of them ever wrote back. Malcolm knew that most hustlers couldn't write a letter or even read one. He had been the smoothest talker in Harlem. Now he was embarrassed by how poorly he expressed himself.

To improve his writing and his vocabulary, he began copying out the dictionary, one page a day. He stepped up his studies in the prison library. He read books on history, religion, philosophy, and science. After "lights out," he read in his cell by a light from the corridor. He read about the history of Africa. He read about the achievements of his own people in America. He read about Europe's colonization of Africa and Asia. And especially, he read the teachings of Elijah Muhammad.

Mr. Muhammad taught that the white man had "whitened" history. That the science of genetics proved that you couldn't get a black man from a white man—you could only get a white man from a black man. That the first humans had appeared in Africa. That great civilizations had emerged in Africa. That the African slave trade was the most monstrous crime in the history of the world. That the white man is the devil. Everything Malcolm read confirmed it.

It all made sense. Once he accepted that one basic idea, all the rest fell into place.

He began talking to other prisoners. He talked about history. He talked about Islam and the Honorable Elijah Muhammad. He took part in prison debates. He discovered the thrill of speaking before an audience. "It was right there in prison," he later wrote, "that I made up my mind to devote the rest of my life to telling the white man about himself—or die."

Prison authorities paroled Malcom in August 1952. He left prison as a man reborn. Gone was "Detroit Red," with his conk and his foul ways. In his place was a Muslim with closely cut hair and a devotion to Allah and his Messenger, Elijah Muhammad.

"Malcolm Little" was gone too. Some months later he would receive a new name. He believed that his true, African name had been stolen from him by the white devils. He could never know what it was. He formally requested a new name from Allah and received it from his Messenger. It was a name shared by many in the Nation of Islam, a name that proudly proclaimed his unknown heritage.

From that day on, he would be "Malcolm X."

CHAPTER 4
For Allah and His Messenger

Elijah Muhammad was a small man with a gentle brown face. Malcolm was not prepared for the power of his feelings upon meeting him in person. Allah's Messenger was describing how the "white devil" had "brainwashed the so-called Negro." Malcolm had read these words many times, but now he was hearing them from the Messenger's own lips. And what Malcolm felt was love, awe, and reverence. This was the man who had saved him. This was the man who had opened his heart to Allah and his mind to truth. This was the true leader of the black people.

It was a Sunday afternoon in September 1952. Malcolm had traveled to Chicago with a group of Muslims from Detroit to hear their leader speak. As he sat there in

Muhammad's Temple Number Two, Elijah Muhammad nodded to him.

"Brother Malcolm," he said. "Will you stand?"

Malcolm rose. The eyes of 200 Muslims were on him. Mr. Muhammad told the audience of Malcolm's letters from prison. He described the life Malcolm had led and how Allah had changed him. The devil might say that Brother Malcolm only used Islam to get out of prison, he said. Now would come the true test. Would Malcolm return to his old ways of drinking, dope, and crime?

"We will see," Mr. Muhammad said. "I believe he is going to remain faithful."

After the meeting, Elijah Muhammad invited Malcolm to be his guest for dinner at his home.

Malcolm had been out of prison for less than a month. On his release, he had gone first to Ella's house in Boston. He stayed there just one night before catching a bus for Detroit. He and Ella agreed that he should start fresh in a city where the police didn't know him. In Detroit, many of Malcolm's sisters and brothers were active in the Nation. His brother Wilfred was managing a furniture store and had promised Malcolm a job.

Before leaving Boston, Malcolm bought a pair of glasses, a suitcase, and a watch. Later, he would reflect that they were symbols of his new life. The glasses were the result of all the reading he had done in dim prison light. The suitcase was a symbol of all the traveling he would do. And the watch was what he would live by.

Elijah Muhammad, leader of the Nation of Islam, later to be called the Black Muslims.

In Harlem, he'd worn an expensive watch just for show. Now he was aware of time ticking away. He had wasted too much of it.

In Detroit, he worked for a while selling furniture in Wilfred's store. The job disgusted him. This store in the black slums was owned by whites. It offered easy credit to the poor African American customers. But it charged high interest, and the furniture was little better than junk. As Malcolm saw it, what little money the black community had was being drained off by the white devil. As soon as he could, he found another job in a garbage-truck factory.

Malcolm lived with Wilfred and his family. They lived a strict Muslim life, praying five times a day. They attended meetings at Temple Number One. It had been founded by W. D. Fard himself. Malcolm was impressed by how well mannered and quiet the members were. The men dressed neatly in plain dark suits. The women wore long white robes and kerchiefs. But the temple was small, and there were many empty seats. This bothered Malcolm. He saw the streets filled with "brainwashed" black people. They drank, fought, cursed, and chased pleasure—all of which kept them under the devil's heel. Some of the members of the temple took the attitude that Allah would bring the people to Islam. Malcolm did not agree. He knew the people in these streets. He felt that Islam should bring Allah to them. When he had dinner with Elijah Muhammad in Chicago, he told him so.

Elijah Muhammad agreed. He told him to go after the young people. The older ones would follow out of shame.

Malcolm took that advice as an order from God himself. Every evening, he walked the streets of Detroit's black slums. "My man, let me pull your coat to something," he would say in the street talk of his hustler days. It meant "let me get your attention." Slowly, the meetings at Temple Number One began to fill up. Before not too long, its membership had tripled.

In the spring of 1953, Malcolm was asked to speak at a meeting. He talked about the life he had led and how Mr. Muhammad's teachings had changed him. The temple's minister was impressed. He asked Malcolm to give a speech to the brothers and sisters of Temple Number One.

It was a message his audience had heard before, but never in such a powerful way. His short, stabbing sentences grabbed everyone's attention. He expressed the rage they all felt with the strength they all wished they had. He told them that they had been brainwashed—as he had been brainwashed. That the white man had made him hate himself for being black. That he had conked his hair to make it straight like the white man's. He called them his *beautiful* black brothers and sisters.

It was the first of many speeches.

He told street audiences that the white man hated them because his guilty conscience couldn't bear the sight of them. He told them that the white man ought to get down on his knees before them and *beg* to be forgiven. But the white man wouldn't do it, he said, because the white man is the devil. Malcolm's voice was constantly hoarse from all the talking he did.

That summer, Malcolm was named assistant minister of Temple Number One. Elijah Muhammad heard about his success. He praised Malcolm and paid him a visit. Malcolm went to Chicago and met with him as often as he could. He met Elijah Muhammad's family: his mother, his wife, and his many children. Malcolm worshipped the man. He also feared him—not as one feared a man with a gun, he would say, but as one feared the power of the sun. Malcolm drew strength from the man's power. Malcolm never failed to tell his street audiences that he owed his soul to this gentle man. He would give up his life for him.

While Malcolm was still in prison, his brother Reginald had been expelled from the Nation for breaking its strict moral code. He had had an affair with a Muslim woman. The news had been a great shock to Malcolm. But when forced to choose between his own brother and Elijah Muhammad, he had chosen to be loyal to Allah's Messenger. He had cut his own brother out of his life. To be a Muslim, one had to give up the sinful life, and Reginald had been too weak.

In Malcolm X, Elijah Muhammad realized he had more than a loyal follower. He had an amazing natural leader who could speak to the troubled black masses. He asked Malcolm to go to Boston to organize a temple there.

At the time, there was only one Muslim brother in Boston. The first meetings were held at his house. He invited a handful of people who were curious about Islam to hear Malcolm speak. Word spread, and more people came to the weekly meetings.

Malcolm would first talk about Elijah Muhammad and his teachings. To demonstrate that the white man was the devil, Malcolm would dramatize the horrors of slavery in chilling detail. "I want you, when you leave this room, to start to *see* all this whenever you see the devil white man. . . . Every time you see a white man . . . think of how it was on your slave foreparents' bloody, sweaty backs that he *built* this empire that's today the richest of all nations!"

Malcolm's old friend Shorty was back in Roxbury. He and Malcolm got together to talk about old times. Shorty had used his time in prison to study music. He had his own band now. But when Malcolm started preaching Islam, Shorty was uncomfortable. He put Malcolm off with jokes.

Laura was in Roxbury too. She was a drug addict and a prostitute. She had been in and out of jail several times. Malcolm felt a terrible shame for what had happened to Laura. He had introduced her to that life—the life of self-hatred he had lived before he found Allah.

Now he was helping other Roxbury blacks find Allah too. Elijah Muhammad called it "fishing"—catching new souls for Islam. He had never had a better fisherman than Malcolm X. Within a few months, Malcolm's speeches had brought in enough followers to establish Temple Number 11 in Boston. He became its minister, but only for a short time. Elijah Muhammad sent him to Philadelphia to start Temple Number 12.

Then, in April 1954, he appointed Malcolm minister of Temple Number Seven in New York City. Malcolm X was going home—to Harlem.

CHAPTER 5

"The Angriest Negro in America"

"Wherever a black man goes, that's Harlem," Malcolm X said. Harlem was black America's national capital. In Harlem, there was enormous despair, rage, strength, and vitality, just waiting for an idea and a leader that could be its voice. Malcolm wanted the black nationalism of Islam to be that idea and Elijah Muhammad to be that leader.

Black nationalism is the idea that blacks should be independent and united. But the Nation was not the only black nationalist group in Harlem, nor did it offer the only solutions. Some black nationalists wanted a separate black nation to be carved out of the United States. Some wanted a return to Africa. Others saw these ideas as idle dreams. They wanted black control of black communities. They urged people to support black-owned businesses and separate black schools. Most black nationalists cared nothing for religion—only the Nation of Islam attempted to give these ideas a religious force.

The Muslim community in New York City at that time was not very large. Temple Number Seven was a storefront in the poorest section of Harlem. Malcolm knew the despair in these streets where he had once sold drugs. Still, his street preaching brought in only a few curious people. He had better luck when he started "working the crowds" at black nationalist rallies. These people were ready to believe any message about the "white devil."

Malcolm's best success came when he talked to people leaving storefront churches. Most of them were from the rural South. They had a strong spiritual base, and they enjoyed good preaching. Those who came to the temple heard a powerful talk about "what this white man's religion called Christianity has done to us." Many looked interested, but few were willing to follow Islam's strict moral code.

Malcolm was upset with his poor results. Elijah Muhammad advised patience. He told him not to set a faster pace than his followers could keep up with. He knew Malcolm was his best minister. He sent him all over the country to preach and to set up new temples. Then in April 1957, something happened that made every African American person in New York take notice of the Nation of Islam and Malcolm X.

On a Harlem street corner, a Muslim named Hinton Johnson saw two white policemen beating up a black suspect. "You're not in Alabama!" Johnson said. "This is New York!" The police ordered him to leave the scene. When he refused, they clubbed him and dragged him off to a police station.

At that time, in every Muslim community there were Muslim businesses. The Nation had started food stores, drugstores, and dry-cleaning shops so that Muslims would not have to shop at white-owned businesses. It also ran restaurants where Islam's strict food laws were observed. The night of Johnson's arrest, someone phoned the Muslim restaurant in Harlem and reported what had happened to him. Within an hour, 50 members of the Fruit of Islam, the Nation's "internal police," were standing outside the police station. Standing up front was Malcolm X.

The 50 members, who were trained in self-defense, stood at attention like soldiers. They were silent and well ordered. Behind them were Muslim sisters in their white kerchiefs. A crowd of about 2,500 people had gathered around them. They were not so well ordered. The police expected trouble.

Then Malcolm X walked up the station steps. He demanded to see Johnson. The police refused. Malcolm announced that he and the Fruit of Islam members would remain outside the station until he could see Brother Hinton and get him to a hospital. As for the rest of the crowd, Malcolm said, they weren't his people and they weren't his problem.

A reporter from an African American newspaper was there. Malcolm knew and trusted him. The reporter offered to let Malcolm and police officials use his office to talk. The officials didn't know Malcolm, and they weren't interested.

"The New York Police Department can handle anything in Harlem," one officer said. "We're not asking for help."

At hearing this, Malcolm walked out. Alarmed, the police officials asked the reporter to bring him back. "All we are asking," Malcolm said, "is to see Brother Hinton. This is all we want. If he's hurt, we want to get him to the hospital. If he isn't, you can go on with your case."

"If we agree, will you get your people out of the street?" the officials asked.

"This is all we ask for, and this is all we want," Malcolm repeated.

Malcolm and the reporter were let in to see Hinton Johnson. His skull had been smashed. He would later have to have a steel plate put in his head. The police gave orders to have him sent to Harlem Hospital. Malcolm went outside and waved his hand. The crowd melted away.

"This," one police official muttered, "is too much power for one man to have."

The story grew in the telling. So did Malcolm's reputation. And so too did Temple Number Seven. One new member later told of hearing "how this man Malcolm X was out front . . . and how the Muslim brothers and sisters reacted. The brotherhood was what attracted me. The unity . . . and love. So I went . . . to seek out the Muslims."

Other people were attracted to Malcolm X, drawn by his message and his personal force. One was a Muslim sister named Betty X. Malcolm was still a bachelor at the age of 33. He admitted to a deep distrust of women. Elijah Muhammad had encouraged him to stay single.

Malcolm noticed Sister Betty for more than a year before he spoke to her. She was a "proper Muslim woman." She had been training as a nurse. But her foster parents had cut off money for her education when they found out she had become a Muslim. When Malcolm X realized that he was seriously thinking about marriage, he told Elijah Muhammad. The leader of the Nation wanted to meet Sister Betty. She went to Chicago, where Mr. Muhammad pronounced her "a fine sister." In January 1958, she and Malcolm were married. Everyone in the Muslim community was amazed.

That year, a black scholar named C. Eric Lincoln wrote a book about the Nation of Islam. He called it *The Black Muslims in America.* In 1959, CBS television ran a news program on black nationalism. Picking up on Lincoln's title, CBS referred to the Nation as "the Black Muslims." It was by this name that most Americans came to know Elijah Muhammad's movement.

The CBS program was called "The Hate that Hate Produced." Its producer was Mike Wallace. The reporter was Louis Lomax, one of TV's first black journalists. Lomax had never heard of Malcolm X when he started his research. But as he talked to people in Harlem about "the Black Muslims," Malcolm's name kept coming up. Lomax arranged a meeting with Malcolm. He asked if he and Elijah Muhammad would agree to be interviewed on camera. As Lomax later told the story, Malcolm thought it would be the best thing that ever happened to the Nation of Islam. He talked Elijah Muhammad into agreeing to the interview.

"The Hate that Hate Produced" shocked white Americans. Few of them had any idea that there were black Americans who felt that way. "Black racism," Mike Wallace called their ideas. "These home-grown Negro-American Muslims . . . claim a membership of at least a quarter of a million. . . . Their [ideas are] being taught in 50 cities. . . . They have their own schools . . . where Muslim children are taught to hate the white man.
. . . Wherever they go, [they] withdraw from the life of the community. They have their own stores, super-markets, barbershops, restaurants. . . ."

The program showed Elijah Muhammad speaking at a mass meeting. White Americans heard for the first time his belief that the white man is the devil and was soon to be destroyed. But it was Malcolm X who made the deepest impression.

"You can go up to any little Muslim child and ask them where is hell and who is the devil," Malcolm said, "and . . . he'll tell you that hell is right here where he's been catching it and . . . that the one who is responsible for him having received this hell is the devil."

After that, the Nation was often in the news. Its membership grew. Its temples were now called *mosques,* following Muslim custom around the world. Muslim rallies filled sports arenas. Most people who joined were the poorest blacks from big-city slums. But some middle-class blacks became Muslims too, and many more admired them. The minister of one mosque was a medical doctor. Another was a former Christian preacher. Educated blacks found a core of truth in the odd history taught by W. D. Fard. Many Africans brought to America as slaves *had* been Muslims. Christianity *did* teach blacks to worship a "white Jesus." And even if one didn't believe that white men were devils, from the way they treated blacks they might as well have been.

Most important, the Nation encouraged black pride and self-respect. And no one represented that pride and self-respect better than Malcolm X. At Muslim rallies, he never failed to say that all honor was due to Allah and his Messenger, the Honorable Elijah Muhammad. When reporters called him "the number two Black Muslim," he was always quick to correct them: "*All* Muslims are number two, after Elijah Muhammad." But it was Malcolm that people came to hear. It was Malcolm that

In the early 1960s, Malcolm started a Muslim newspaper, Muhammad Speaks, *that helped spread his message throughout America.*

reporters wanted to interview. It was Malcolm that colleges wanted on their speakers' programs. He started a Muslim newspaper, which he called *Muhammad Speaks.* However, the words in the paper were mostly Malcolm's.

He never missed a chance to get his message to America. And what he said was frightening to many whites. This was the time of the civil rights movement in the South. African American leaders such as Dr. Martin Luther King, Jr., were fighting for justice and equality through nonviolent protest. There was nothing non-violent about Malcolm X. He said that blacks should defend themselves "by any means necessary." Dr. King supported *integration,* open and equal relations between the races. Malcolm said that this was impossible in racist America. Integration meant white control. It meant blacks being treated as the white man's children. Stirring cream into his coffee, Malcolm would joke, "coffee is the only thing I like integrated."

The black masses didn't want integration, Malcolm said. They didn't want to live with white people or marry white people. They wanted escape from self-hatred. They wanted respect as human beings. They wanted not to be penned up in slums. They wanted not to be looked at as dirt. When asked what was the best thing whites could do to support the black struggle, Malcolm said, "Stay out of the black man's sight."

Black leaders who opposed Malcolm were embarrassed by him, but there were none who could out-debate him.

Malcolm used evidence of southern brutality in the fight against the civil rights movement to make his point that peaceful integration was impossible in a racist America.

Few were foolish enough even to try. He insulted blacks who defended the white man. One black leader criticized Malcolm for speaking "too emotionally" and for refusing to condemn violence.

A talk-show host asked whether it was true that Malcolm was "the angriest Negro in America."

"That is correct, sir," Malcolm replied.

CHAPTER 6
Silenced

In 1960, Malcolm visited Africa. He was in Egypt during the *hajj*, the sacred Muslim journey to the holy city of Mecca. It is likely that he saw Muslims of all races passing through on their way to Mecca. Malcolm was well aware that traditional Islam is not concerned with race, and does not preach that black people are victims of "white devils."

After a TV talk-show appearance in Los Angeles, Malcolm was surrounded by angry Arab students. They were white. They accused him of teaching a "false Islam." Malcolm explained that he used such language as "white devils" to "wake up" black Americans. He did not mean any individual white man, but the historical record of the white race. The Arabs found this an empty argument. Malcolm refused to publicly discuss the issue any further.

It's possible that he did this out of respect for Elijah Muhammad. The man had saved his soul. The Nation of Islam was bringing self-respect to hundreds of thousands of African Americans. And what were they responding to? Not Allah, not the pure Muslim life, but the message that "the white man is the devil." To preach a nonracial Islam then could have destroyed the movement. Its followers would have been left with nothing to believe in.

By 1961, Elijah Muhammad was in poor health. Asthma often left him gasping for breath. Black Muslims began thinking the unthinkable: What would happen when Allah's Messenger died? Malcolm heard stories. People were accusing him of trying to "take over." They said he was "taking credit" for the Messenger's ideas. They said that he had made a lot of money from his speaking tours.

Malcolm shrugged the stories off. Mr. Muhammad had warned him that people would be jealous of him. No one was more loyal to the Nation of Islam than Malcolm X. Surely Mr. Muhammad knew that. In 1962, he appointed Malcolm national minister of the Nation of Islam. It officially made him the acting leader of the Nation. It suggested that Muhammad wanted him to be the leader after he was dead.

A minister named John Ali, however, thought he should be the next leader. Some of Muhammad's sons were also jealous of Malcolm. One son, Herbert, was now editor of *Muhammad Speaks*. During the year 1962, the paper printed fewer and fewer stories about Malcolm X. Malcolm heard another hard-to-believe rumor: Elijah Muhammad had *ordered* his son to print as little as possible about Malcolm's activities. Then suddenly Malcolm was excluded from the paper completely.

While this was happening, there was still plenty of news about Malcolm X in the national and world press. Thousands attended his rallies in Harlem and other places. But then the Nation ordered him to stop staging large rallies. Elijah Muhammad told him to stay off TV news shows.

What was going on? Malcolm suspected that John Ali and another man, Raymond Sharrieff, had turned the Messenger against him. Sharrieff was married to Elijah Muhammad's daughter. He was supreme captain of the Fruit of Islam. Malcolm had criticized this internal police group. He had heard stories of them beating up other Muslims for not making contributions or for not selling enough copies of *Muhammad Speaks*.

Malcolm still thought his personal ties with Mr. Muhammad would overcome such differences. But by then rumors about the Messenger himself were flying again. Several of his young, unmarried secretaries had become pregnant. They had been suspended under the Nation's strict moral code. Now two of them were naming Muhammad himself as the father of their children! Muslims were leaving the Chicago mosque in disgust. Some were calling Allah's Messenger a hypocrite, for preaching the moral life while taking Muslim sisters as his lovers. Non-Muslims were asking Malcolm whether the rumors were true.

Malcolm had heard similar rumors about Elijah Muhammad's misconduct as far back as 1955. He had refused to believe them then. This was the man who had brought him to Allah. This was the man who had expelled Malcolm's brother Reginald for that very sin.

Now Malcolm was forced to face this issue once again, and he had doubts. He was more troubled than at any time since his prison days. He flew to Chicago. He sought out Wallace Muhammad, the Messenger's second son and the one Malcolm most respected. Wallace knew why he had come. He discouraged Malcolm from talking directly to his father.

Next, Malcolm met with the women who had made the charges. He broke the Muslim rule against talking to suspended members. The women told him that the rumors were true. They also reported something else: though Mr. Muhammad had called Malcolm X the greatest minister he had ever had, he had also called him "dangerous." Some day, Allah's Messenger had said, Malcolm would turn against him.

Malcolm was stunned and hurt. His leader had been praising him to his face but had been calling him disloyal behind his back.

The only thing to do, Malcolm decided, was to talk to Elijah Muhammad. To be silent was as bad as being disloyal. If the news became public, the Nation of Islam could be destroyed.

Malcolm wrote to Mr. Muhammad. He told him frankly about the stories he had heard. Muhammad phoned him in New York. He said that he would discuss the matter with Malcolm when he next saw him.

That meeting took place in April 1963 in Phoenix, Arizona, where Muhammad was recovering from his asthma. Allah's Messenger did not deny his sin. He had done it to fulfill a prophecy, he explained. In the Bible, David had taken another man's wife. Noah had gotten drunk. Elijah Muhammad claimed that he *was* David, *was* Noah, and had to do these things.

Malcolm stopped talking about morality in his speeches. He began teaching that a man's closeness to God outweighed his human weaknesses. He talked to other ministers about what they might do should the stories about Elijah Muhammad become public knowledge. Word of these private conversations got back to Elijah Muhammad.

By 1963, Martin Luther King and his ideas about integration between the races were making headlines across the country. King's campaign that year in Birmingham, Alabama, focused the country's attention on the nonviolent movement. Birmingham was a symbol of *segregation*, the forced and unequal separation of the races. King's people marched through the city's streets. They were beaten and jailed. They were set upon by police dogs and sprayed with fire hoses.

Malcolm X saw no point to it. King was sending children out to be beaten, he said. What sort of a man did that? And for what end? For the right to sit at lunch counters with white people? The civil rights movement had no meaning for blacks in the North. They already had the right to sit at lunch counters with white people. What they didn't have was decent jobs, decent housing, or respect.

In August 1963, more than 200,000 people gathered in Washington, D.C. They marched in support of civil rights laws and peace between the races. They sang songs like "We Shall Overcome." They heard Dr. King give a speech about his dream of an America free of racism.

Malcolm X called it the "farce on Washington." Dr. King might have a dream, but black people in America were living a nightmare. They weren't going to win their freedom by marching and singing.

As for the "progress" that had been made by the civil rights movement, Malcolm couldn't see any. "For four hundred years the white man has had his foot-long knife in the black man's back," he said. "Now he starts to wiggle the knife out, maybe six inches. We're supposed to be grateful? Why, if the white man *jerked* the knife out, it's *still* going to leave a scar!"

On November 22, 1963, President John F. Kennedy was murdered in Dallas, Texas. Within hours, every Muslim minister received word from Elijah Muhammad. They were told to say nothing at all about the assassination. If pressed by a reporter, they were to answer, "No comment."

Elijah Muhammad had been scheduled to speak in New York that week. A few days before Kennedy's death, he had canceled his appearance and asked Malcolm to speak in his place. Only weeks earlier, he and Malcolm had stood together at a Muslim rally. Elijah Muhammad had hugged Malcolm X. "This is my most faithful, hardworking minister," he had said. "He will follow me until the day he dies."

In New York, shortly after the assassination, Malcolm spoke on a favorite theme. He talked about how the white man would "reap what he had sowed." As he practiced violence, so would he be the victim of violence. After the speech, there was a question-and-answer period. The first question Malcolm was asked was what he thought about the Kennedy assassination.

Malcolm answered without thinking. "[It was] a case of the chickens coming home to roost," he said. He was talking about America as a violent country. He meant that the violence and hate of white America had now struck down its leader. But that wasn't how it looked in the headlines. It looked as though Malcolm X was saying that the assassination was a good thing.

The next day, Malcolm met with Elijah Muhammad. The Muslim leader criticized Malcolm's statement. The country was in mourning for President Kennedy, he said. Such a statement made the Nation of Islam look bad. Then he ordered Malcolm X silenced for 90 days.

Malcolm was numb from shock. But he submitted to his leader's discipline. On the flight home, he wondered how he would tell his assistants at Mosque Number Seven. When he arrived, he learned that they'd already been told.

Every newspaper in New York had also been told, as had every radio and TV station. And the order silencing him not only concerned talking to the press, Malcolm found out. He was not even to teach in his own mosque.

The next day, the Nation of Islam issued a statement. It said that Minister Malcolm X would be reinstated in 90 days, "if he submits."

All of Malcolm's old hustler instincts warned him that he was being set up. *If he submits?* He had already submitted. The statement made it sound as if he were rebelling.

Then in February 1964, near the end of his term of silence, Malcolm began to hear new rumors. He heard that certain Muslim brothers had been ordered to kill him. And he knew that there was only one man with the power to give or approve such an order.

CHAPTER 7

A New Direction

For Malcolm, it was as though something in nature had gone wrong. It was as though the sun had stopped shining or the earth had stopped turning.

He had received death threats before. They had come from white "hate groups," such as the Ku Klux Klan and the American Nazi party. But now a member of his own mosque was telling him at the risk of his own life that he had been ordered to kill Malcolm.

Other Muslims had been forbidden to speak to Malcolm. It was clear that Elijah Muhammad meant to expel him. Malcolm's life since he left prison had been devoted to the Nation of Islam. To be expelled from the movement would be like being sent back there. And now the man who had lifted him up wanted him dead. The thought nearly drove him crazy.

It was Cassius Clay who lifted him up this time. The Muslim boxer, who would soon change his name to

Muhammad Ali, was in Florida, training for his heavy-weight title fight against Sonny Liston. He invited Malcolm and his family to be his guests.

It was a large family by then. Malcolm and Betty had four daughters. He was happy for a chance to spend some relaxed time with them.

He visited Clay at his training camp. They had met at the Detroit mosque in 1962. They had become friends, even though the Nation of Islam did not approve of sports. Boxing experts gave Clay no chance of beating the powerful champion Liston. Only he and Malcolm X seemed to believe he could win. Before the fight, they prayed together in Clay's dressing room. When Clay won the title that night, no one was happier than Malcolm.

Yet two weeks later, when Malcolm formally broke with the Nation of Islam, Ali chose to stick with Elijah Muhammad.

Back in New York, Malcolm was trying to figure out what to do. He was fearing for his life. There were Black Muslims everywhere. Any one of them might shoot him if he believed Allah—or Allah's Messenger—wanted it done.

Malcolm tried to think of a way for him to continue both as a Muslim and as a leader in the black people's struggle for human rights. Non-Muslims as well as Muslims respected him. Middle-class blacks as well as the poor were stirred by him. Even many whites admired him, despite the fact that he had called them devils.

The group he saw as "his" people, however, were the black masses in the cities. They knew he was one leader who would never sell them out to the white man. They had no power, but it was their very powerlessness that made them dangerous. They had nothing to lose. It was why so many of them were drawn to the hustler's life. They had given up on making it in the white man's world. They were frustrated and angry. They had no respect for community or religion. They had no sense of right and wrong. If touched off, they could be a violent, destructive force. But if they were organized and had a sense of purpose, they could change the direction of their lives.

Power in America, Malcolm knew, came from money and political strength. The black masses had little money. But if they used what they had to build and support black businesses, the community could prosper. As for political strength, there were about 20 million African Americans in the United States. If they voted as a bloc, as other interest groups did, they could decide elections. They could form a solid group that whites couldn't push around.

Malcolm knew he couldn't just stand alone and say "follow me." He needed an organization, a program. It would have to be based on black nationalism. It would have to take Islam's position against unclean living while welcoming non-Muslims as well. It would have to *practice* what he felt the Nation of Islam only preached.

In March 1964, Malcolm X called a press conference. He announced that he had been forced out of the Nation of Islam. He was starting his own organization, called Muslim Mosque, Inc. Its goal was black independence, "with our people going back home, to our own African homeland." But in the short term, he said, "we want to get the best type of life out of our own community as we can."

Muslim Mosque, Inc., would have many of the same goals as the Nation of Islam. It would seek black independence and pride through hard work and moral living. At least 50 former members of the Nation were coming with him. But for the first time, Malcolm offered to work with other black leaders too. "As of this minute," he said with a big smile, "I've forgotten everything bad [they've] said about me. And I pray that they can also forget the many bad things I've said about them." Muslim Mosque, Inc., would be for blacks only. But whites of good conscience were welcome to contribute money and ideas.

Over the next few weeks, Malcolm announced no clear plan of action for his new group. He spoke strongly for armed self-defense and "revolution." Yet he seemed more interested in building up black economic power. "Any time you have to rely on your enemy for a job, you're in bad shape," he said. Before, he had never had any use for voting. Now he spoke of winning power through the political system. He talked about the choice blacks had between "the ballot or the bullet." He told followers that it was not too late to win freedom through the ballot. But he said, whites had to know that blacks were ready to use the bullet if they had to.

Meanwhile, Malcolm sought peace with the Nation of Islam. The Nation would not have it. Elijah Muhammad called him a hypocrite. "He broke with me, I didn't break with him," Muhammad said. Malcolm's own brother, Philbert X, compared him to Judas and called him "crazy." The Nation sued Malcolm to get back the house where he lived, which the Nation claimed it owned.

Malcolm was still a Muslim, even if he was no longer a "Black Muslim." He was a religious man. He wanted respect as a Muslim minister, as Dr. King had respect as a Christian minister. He sought out a man named Youssouf Shawarbi. He was an Egyptian professor, learned in Islam, who was teaching in New York. "I want to learn about the real Islam," Malcolm told him.

Malcolm studied with Shawarbi for several weeks. The Egyptian taught him verses from the Koran. One of them read, "Muslims are all brothers regardless of their color and race." He taught Malcolm that Arabs sometimes thought they were better than other Muslims because the prophet Muhammad was an Arab. But this was not what Allah taught. "You are all the rulers and the ruled," the Koran said. Allah would judge men by their deeds, not what nation they came from. These ideas, Shawarbi noticed, seemed to move Malcolm deeply.

In March 1964, Malcolm broke with the Nation of Islam and announced a willingness to work with other black leaders. That same month he joined Dr. Martin Luther King and other civil rights leaders in Washington to watch the debate in Congress over the civil rights bill.

Some traditional Muslims were unhappy about the time Shawarbi was spending with Malcolm. They didn't think Malcolm really believed in a "color-blind" Islam. They suspected that he was using the Egyptian professor as a step toward his real goal: to be seen as *the* Muslim minister to black America. Shawarbi was said to hold "the key to Mecca." All Muslims who are able are required at least once in their lifetime to make the pilgrimage to the holy city. No American could get permission to make the hajj without a letter from Shawarbi confirming that he was a true Muslim. Some people felt that this was all Malcolm was after.

In fact, Malcolm did want to make the hajj. But Shawarbi believed he was sincere. He gave Malcolm the letter he needed.

Malcolm was broke. To get money for plane fare and hotels, he went to an old source—his sister Ella. She had surprised him in 1961 by joining the Nation of Islam. Later, she had quit and joined a traditional Muslim group. She had even started a school where Arabic was taught. Ella had gone her own way, but she admired her brother. She loaned him money she had been saving for her own hajj.

On April 13, 1964, Malcolm X left on his holy journey. He spent two days in Egypt before going on to Jedda, Saudi Arabia, the "gateway" to Mecca. The hajj involved several days of prayer. For Malcolm, every moment and every feeling was an amazing experience.

When Malcolm finally visited the holy city of Mecca, what he found there shocked him. He saw tens of thousands of pilgrims from all over the world. They were of all colors, from blue-eyed, blonde whites, to black-skinned Africans. These worshippers showed a togetherness of spirit that Malcolm would never have believed possible between black and white people.

What Malcolm witnessed in Mecca convinced him more than ever that Islam was the one religion that could solve the race problem. He felt that true Islam removes racism, because its followers bow down to Allah and accept each other as brothers and sisters, regardless of color.

After his hajj, Malcolm went to Africa. He visited Nigeria and Ghana. Everywhere he went, people knew of him. Heads of state treated him as an honored guest. He spoke at universities. Students were interested in the black Americans' struggle for freedom. They told him of their own recently won fight for independence and their efforts to build their new nations.

In Ghana, he met African Americans who had gone to live in their ancient homeland. The writers Julian Mayfield and Maya Angelou showed him the sights. Malcolm seemed to want to cover himself in all that was African. He took hundreds of pictures. "He wanted to look at everything," Angelou later remembered.

Malcolm returned home on May 21 with a new Muslim name: El-Hajj Malik El-Shabazz. The first part, *El-Hajj,* honored him as one who had been to Mecca. The second, *Malik,* was taken from *Malcolm,* but also means "king" in Arabic. And the third was from the name of his tribe, *Shabazz,* as taught by W. D. Fard and Elijah Muhammad.

Malcolm was greeted by a large crowd at the airport. His family was there. Cheering supporters were there. So were reporters, who wanted to know about this "new Malcolm X." He assured them that while he had learned to accept white Muslims as his brothers, he could not feel that way about white Americans.

"No matter how much respect [they] show towards me," he said, ". . . as long as it is not shown to every one of our people in this country, it doesn't exist for me." He announced an agreement he had reached with African leaders. Together they would bring a case in the United Nations against white America for violating black people's human rights.

For El-Hajj Malik El-Shabazz, white men were no longer devils. For Malcolm X, white racists were still the enemy.

CHAPTER 8
A Time for Martyrs

On July 16, 1964, a white policeman shot a black teenager in Harlem. Two nights later, an angry crowd gathered in front of the local police station. They demanded the officer's arrest for murder. Instead, the police started arresting people in the crowd. The people scattered through the streets, smashing store windows, looting, and setting fires.

It was not the first time Harlem's people had burned down their community in frustration and rage. It had happened in 1935. It happened again in 1943, when "Detroit Red" was living there.

The Harlem riot of 1964 lasted four days. The police could do nothing to stop it. Only one person, possibly, could have stopped it. The angry crowds called for him to lead them. They gathered in the streets and shouted, "Malcolm! We want Malcolm! Wait till Malcolm comes!"

But Malcolm X was not in Harlem. He was in Cairo,

Egypt, at a meeting of the Organization of African Unity (OAU). On June 28, Malcolm had announced the formation of the Organization of Afro-American Unity (OAAU). He called on blacks to put aside their differences and work together for unity and freedom "by any means necessary."

The OAAU would organize rent strikes, school boycotts, and voter registration drives. It would support programs to improve housing for blacks and to help black youth avoid the hustler's life. It would make war on gangsters who sold drugs in the black slums. It would launch a cultural program "to unbrainwash an entire people." And it would seek the unity of black people around the world.

This idea had a name: *Pan-Africanism.* It was Pan-Africanism that was behind Malcolm's message to the OAU leaders. Black Americans were their long-lost brothers and sisters, Malcolm told them. Their problem was a world problem, a problem of human rights. "We [ask] the independent African states to help us bring our problem before the United Nations, on the grounds that the United States . . . is morally incapable of protecting the lives and property of 20 million African Americans. And on the grounds that our [worsening situation] is . . . becoming a threat to world peace. . . ."

Young African Americans, Malcolm explained, were no longer willing to be patient. They were ready to defend themselves against their oppressors, "no matter what the odds against us are. . . .

"In the interest of world peace, . . . we [ask] the heads of . . . African states to recommend an immediate investigation into our problem by the United Nations Commission on Human Rights."

The violence in New York and other American cities that summer seemed to underline Malcolm's point. But the investigation never happened.

Malcolm charmed and impressed Africa's leaders. They received him as an ambassador of America's black people. Still Malcolm could gather no real support for his investigation. The nations of the OAU wanted America's friendship. Privately, they praised Malcolm. Publicly, they praised the United States for having just passed the Civil Rights Act of 1964.

Everywhere he went in Africa, Malcolm was followed by agents of the U.S. government. The State Department and the Justice Department were watching his activities. They made Malcolm nervous. One black American he met in Kenya described him as "uncomfortable." When he became sick one night, he was sure he had been poisoned.

At home, the OAAU was attracting little support. Malcolm's program was confusing. He offered no clear plan. "[He] was a lot better at stirring up people than organizing people," one supporter said later. He had

In July 1964, Malcom visited Cairo, Egypt to meet with Muslim leaders and to seek the support of the Organization of African Unity (OAU).

invited other black leaders to join him, but none did. Many were still angry with him for having insulted them years before, comparing them with slaves who had loved their masters. As for the black masses, many admired Malcolm X, but few joined his organizations. And few were really eager to take up arms against white power.

In June, Malcolm had faced the Nation of Islam in court over its suit to take his house. On the witness stand, he revealed what he knew about Elijah Muhammad and his "nine wives." From that day on, there could be no peace between Malcolm X and Elijah Muhammad. There were confrontations and street fights between Malcolm's followers and the Black Muslims. On July 5, as he was entering his car, Malcolm saw four black men armed with knives coming at him. He escaped by speeding away. "Right now," he said at a rally that evening, "things are pretty hot for me." When he left for Africa on July 9, he hoped things would cool off while he was gone.

He stayed until November, much longer than he had planned. He came home to find his new organization in trouble. His people were fighting over which direction they should take. And Malcolm was of little help. He could not decide himself which was the right direction for his movement. He just wanted some results—soon. But his supporters began to disobey his instructions and drift away.

The situation with the Nation of Islam had not cooled off. Malcolm received death threats at his home. Minister Louis X, once a friend, wrote in *Muhammad Speaks* that Malcolm was "now the target of both [his] own followers (which are very few) and the followers of Muhammad. . . . Such a man as Malcolm is worthy of death." Some of Malcolm's followers were badly beaten by members of the Fruit of Islam. Malcolm saw enemies everywhere. He told people that he believed he didn't have long to live.

He didn't stay long in one place that winter. He gave dozens of speeches. In early February, he was in Selma, Alabama, where Martin Luther King was leading a voting rights drive. Dr. King was in jail when Malcolm told his followers, "I'm 100 percent for the effort being made by the black folks here. I believe they have an absolute right to use whatever means are necessary to gain the vote. But I don't believe in nonviolence—no." He turned to Dr. King's wife, who was sitting beside him on the speakers' platform. He told her he hoped he hadn't made her husband's job harder by coming to Selma. He had wanted to make it easier—by "showing white people what the alternative is."

Then he was off again. He went to London, where he met with a group of African leaders. Then he flew to Paris, where he was scheduled to make a speech. French police met him at the airport. They had an order to send him out of the country as an "undesirable." He was home in New York for just a few hours when someone threw two gasoline bombs through the window of his house. He and Betty, who was pregnant with twins, barely managed to get the children outside through the smoke and flames.

The Black Muslims said that Malcolm had done it himself, as a publicity stunt. It was the same thing white racists said about civil rights workers whose houses were burned in Mississippi.

Malcolm now expected to be killed at any time. He saw the Black Muslims as working with the police to "get him." He accused the Nation of Islam of plotting with white hate groups. Because of what had happened in France, he suspected the U.S. government as well.

Publicly, however, he blamed "that man in Chicago"—the man he had once worshipped as Allah's Messenger. In his last interview, on Friday, February 19, he spoke of his time with the Nation of Islam with regret. He claimed he had been "hypnotized and pointed in a certain direction and told to march." He said he was glad to be free of all the pain of his association with Elijah Muhammad's group. And he seemed to accept his fate—even if that fate was death.

"It's a time for martyrs now," he said. "And if I'm to be one, it will be in the cause of brotherhood."

Two days later, on Sunday, February 21, 1965, Malcolm was scheduled to speak at the Audubon Ballroom in Harlem. At 2:00 P.M., he stepped onto the stage and gave a traditional Muslim greeting. At that moment, a fight broke out between two men in the audience. Malcolm held up his hand. "Hold it, hold it, brothers, let's be cool," he said.

Then a man in the front row stood up. He pulled a sawed-off shotgun from under his coat and fired into Malcolm's chest. Two other men with handguns rushed the stage. They shot bullet after bullet into Malcolm X's body.

There was chaos. Everyone was screaming and shouting and running. One gunman was pulled down and beaten. The others disappeared into the crowd.

Malcolm X was dead before he could be taken to a hospital.

The police arrested three men. They were all convicted of murder and sent to prison. Of course, the Nation of Islam was blamed for the killing. But the man captured at the scene, Talmadge Hayer, was not a Black Muslim. The two men picked up later, Norman Butler and Thomas Johnson, were members of the Nation, but it was never proved that they knew Hayer. The question of who ordered the murder of Malcolm X remained a mystery.

Within months, Malcolm's legend began. Black people all over America were wearing "Malcolm X" T-shirts and buttons. Under Malcolm's picture were the words, OUR SHINING BLACK PRINCE. Late in 1965, his autobiography was published. It sold and sold. It was the story of a man who had suffered under white oppression and had beaten it. He had beaten the devil—and beaten him so completely he didn't need to hate him any more.

"They say he taught hate," Malcolm's widow remarked in 1993. "He didn't teach hate; he taught people to love themselves."

Elijah Muhammad died in 1975. The Nation of Islam lives on. It has "forgiven" Malcolm X and today claims him again as one of its own. But many more African Americans, after Malcolm's example, have chosen to follow traditional Islam.

And more still have chosen to follow Malcolm.

Acknowledgements

The publisher and the author wish to acknowledge that the following sources were used for background information in the preparation of this biography.

Breitman, George, *Malcolm Speaks.* New York: Grove Press, 1965.

Goldman, Peter, *The Death and Life of Malcolm X.* New York: Harper and Row, 1973.

Haley, Alex, and Malcolm X, *The Autobiography of Malcolm X.* New York: Random House, 1965.

Lomax, Louis E., *To Kill a Black Man.* Los Angeles: Holloway House, 1967

Rummel, Jack, *Malcolm X: Militant Black Leader.* New York: Chelsea House, 1989.

X, Malcolm, *Malcolm X on Afro-American History.* New York: Pathfinder Press, 1967.

X, Malcolm, *Malcolm X: The Final Speeches.* New York: Pathfinder Press, 1992.